Follow Your Purpose

Career Direction for Students and Prospective Students

DR. TITA L. GRAY

San Diego, CA

Published by

Montezuma Publishing
Aztec Shops Ltd.
San Diego State University
San Diego, California 92182-1701

619-594-7552

www.montezumapublishing.com

ISBN: 978-0-7442-1673-8

Publishing Manager: Kim Mazyck

Design and Layout: Lia Dearborn and Tita L. Gray

Formatting: Lia Dearborn

Cover Design: Lia Dearborn

Quality Control: Jasmine Baiz and Joshua Segui

Contents

Foreword

It was the spring of 2014. I was in my last semester and set to graduate with a degree in Business Management with a Specialization in Entrepreneurship from San Diego State University. I was sitting towards the back of the class waiting for Professor Gray (now Dr. Gray) to come in for the Leadership in Organizations course. I had never heard of Dr. Gray, and frankly, was expecting a professor like all the rest. Luckily, Dr. Gray was not at all like the rest.

I was able to tell almost instantly after she walked into the classroom with her unmistakable aura and warm greeting that she was someone special. I could tell that she was excited to be there. Without her even knowing my name, who I was, or what I wanted to become I could tell that she genuinely wanted to make me better. I watched her approach every single student, colleague, and guest in her classroom that same way. So I knew that my new professor cared, and was genuinely excited about what she was doing. BUT, did she know her stuff?

Throughout that semester I was able to absorb applicable knowledge directly from Dr. Gray that I simply had never been given before. At that point in my college career my brain was pumped full of theories, principles, and business Xs and Os. Dr. Gray was able to take her vast knowledge of those aspects of business and relate them to the art of communication and leadership of people.

On graduation day I was happy to see that Dr. Gray was one of the professors dressed in cap and gown to celebrate with us students. She had no idea at that point how big of an impact she made on my life. I was a 22 year old kid with big dreams of owning successful businesses. Almost immediately after graduation I went to work on building Uncle Bob's Sports Bar & Grill in Temecula, CA. We did most of the construction ourselves building a bar and restaurant from the ground up. After a little more than a year, we opened in 2015. Since the day I graduated I have essentially handled all aspects of the business as an owner-operator.

The greatest gift that Dr. Gray gave me was a confidence to follow my passion. During my semester with her I shared my hopes and dreams. She not only assured me that they could become reality, she showed me the way to get there, much like this book does. I looked forward to her classes every Tuesday and Thursday. I was excited to have conversations with her about the importance of self-awareness, strategy, and life. I very often heard her voice in my head when I was working 130 hour weeks with no income, when I was leading people that were double my age, or when I was negotiating pricing with an industry veteran.

On the last day of class Dr. Gray told us, "Now go out into the world and make your impact. Trust in yourself and what you can do." Without her confidence in me I am not sure if I would have taken the leap of owning and operating a business the way that I did. That is a gift that I simply cannot repay. I am proud to say that we were recently voted the best sports bar in Riverside County by Fox Sports, and are now looking at multiple locations for expansion. Every time a new leap is ahead of me I can still hear Dr. Gray's voice telling me to trust in myself, and go make my impact.

So, trust in Dr. Gray, trust in yourself, and go make your impact.

Ryan Craig
Owner, Uncle Bob's Sports Bar & Grill

Introduction

AWAKENING

*I walked a path of uncertainty
my steps were filled with trepidation,
my purpose contained,
when I looked around for those who told me I
wouldn't, shouldn't, and couldn't, they were no longer
there, only a reflection of myself still following a dream
that wasn't mine.*

Tita L. Gray

Are you a student that wants help with deciding on the best major or career direction? Are you unhappy with your job and want something more meaningful in your life? Maybe you are contemplating a career change and are unsure how to start the process. Welcome, you have chosen the right book.

There are very rational and understandable reasons why people choose majors not necessarily true to their personality. Choosing a career or making a career change can be extremely stressful. At times this process can take months or even years to land that dream job. During career exploration it is important to have the support of your loved ones or friends. While this can be beneficial, your decisions must also be based on your *understanding of who you are and industry trends of the future.*

Normally when I ask a student what industry they want to work in or are interested in they don't have a clue. It's because, in my opinion, we approach career decision-making the wrong way. Customarily, we begin with the selection of a major. I don't blame anyone—it's just how things have always been done. Instead, what if we made it mandatory for everyone in their first and/or second year of college to learn about their field of interest? This could be achieved by employing mandatory internships, conducting informal interviews of people in the selected career, or shadowing existing professionals at their work. I believe that these experiences would assist students at making more informed choices. Additionally, transfer students might find that their time to graduation will shorten due to the decrease of time involved in switching of majors.

The foundation for career decision begins long before a student enters college and is influenced, and even at times dictated, by family, friends, and mentors (Workman, 2015). We often make choices based on what other people believe is right for us. Complete reliance on others complicates the decision-making process because it is impossible to please everyone. The key is to be able to purposefully and knowledgeably articulate your career decisions. That starts by having an understanding of self. In our life journey, we will not always make decisions that are a good fit or seemingly right for us at the time. We often make informed decisions based on the choices, options, and information that were present at the time. Regardless of the outcome of your career choice, being self-aware and self-reliant are critical to how you adapt and navigate your career transition.

My Career Change

In 2012 I left a corporate job to pursue a career in academia. Within a month of moving to San Diego a good friend called and said, "Hey, I know that you want to teach. Why don't you take my place speaking at an event at San Diego State University? Maybe you'll make some connections." Unbeknownst to me, taking his place would lead me to fulfilling a lifelong dream and ambition of becoming an educator and administrator in post-secondary education. That presentation led to my introduction to an amazing faculty member and then a department chair, which led to landing a position as an adjunct faculty member. Prior to beginning my first semester teaching, I called my mentor and former professor at San Francisco State University, Aaron Anderson, and asked him for advice. I specifically asked him because I was one of his first students and I remember some of his highs and lows. His advice was "Be yourself, they'll love you. This is your purpose and passion in life." He was correct and his guidance, teaching, love, and friendship will remain with me forever. (RIP Dr. Anderson)

Although it took 25 years to get here, being an educator was always a strong part of my DNA—I just didn't pursue it initially. We all make career choices for different reasons. Sometimes it's for the monetary gain, peer pressure, family influence or, in my case, lack of self and career awareness. My success has always been circumstantial and most of the time it was unplanned. I just tried to be the best that I could at anything that I did. Most of the time I did not work in an environment that fed my passion and soul; it was just a job. It was not until I made a firm decision to pursue my dream, my purpose, and my passion, that my life changed in ways unimaginable.

Book Purpose

The main premise of this book is to help you find your purpose before graduating and to encourage you to be intentional with your career journey. In addition, it's to encourage and reignite in mature adults the dreams that are instilled in you. Many of us have a dream, hobby, or something we love that can tell us a lot about ourselves. For example, I have never considered myself a writer, but I'm in love with words. I love the meaning, I love the sound, I like how they can connect a story or add emphasis. Not surprising then that writing poetry and stories was always something that provided me with a lot of comfort and reflection. It was my source of self-awareness, self-actualization, and connection. The intent of this book is for you to pay more attention to YOU. It's for you to view life and what you need from it more holistically. Time, knowledge, and purpose are precious and should not be wasted or taken for granted. They are the foundations of what shape a meaningful career. This book is to encourage you to think differently about how you approach career decision making.

There is a distinct difference between building a career and having a job. When you land in an industry that you feel a strong connection with, you can see the vast opportunities ahead of you. You can see yourself as a senior officer or becoming an entrepreneur in that field. You can see yourself making a difference and possibly continuing your education to further your career trajectory. As a result of never giving up on my dream of being a professor, and having friends and colleagues who believed in me, I began the career I always longed for in education. That opportunity led to my appointment as an Assistant Dean, completing a doctorate degree, and writing a book to give back to others for everything that has been given to me.

Dr. Tita Gray

One

3 Circle Concept (3CC)

*"Example is not the main thing in influencing others.
It is the only thing." — Albert Schweitzer*

I developed the 3 Circle Concept (3CC) as a result of continuous career-oriented conversations with students who were primarily college juniors and seniors. Consistently, these students were unsure and uncertain of their career paths and they were experiencing much anxiety and fear as they came closer to graduating. Upon meeting I would ask them "In what industry do you plan to work?" Usually I would get a dead stare or an answer that conveyed no knowledge of a defined industry. I began drawing three circles to illustrate Industries, Companies, and Jobs, which inadvertently became the subject of this book.

The 3 Circle Concept begins with understanding the big picture first— what industry do you want to work in? Is it health, environmental, entertainment, aviation, tourism, financial services, manufacturing, energy, government, education, automotive, etc.? Why is it important to identify your industry first? Because it affects the environment you want to work in and your career trajectory. An individual can get a job almost anywhere, but who aspires to be a manager, director, or vice president in an environment they are not excited about? You might stay for the money or complacency, but you will not be fulfilled with purpose and meaning.

Throughout the chapters of this book, I lay out a very basic yet profound concept with stories, examples, and in-depth discussions on industries. There are key points that must be discussed before we get there.

The first step in career planning and preparation should begin with self-awareness. When you are guided and encouraged, you will be able to make career choices congruent with your personal requirements. When career selection is made inaccurately, time and energy will be wasted until a more fulfilling career is found. Therefore, career counseling is crucial to help you become more aware and make informed decisions about the different fields and available career opportunities that best suit your personality.

As shown in the 3CC illustration below, when students are asked to pick their major they are looking at their career path through a small lens circled by vast choices. The key is to start by reviewing industries first and strategically moving toward a major.

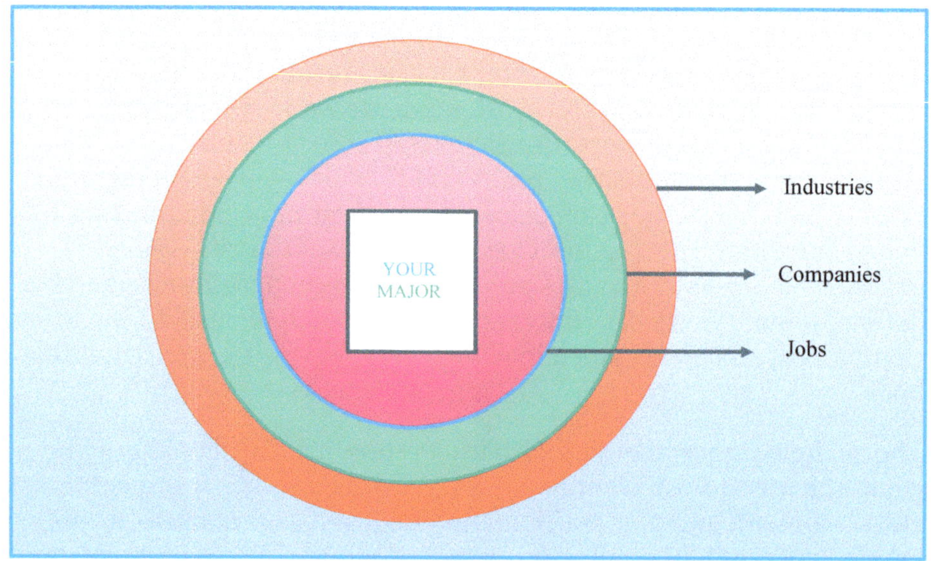

3 Circle Concept (3CC), by Dr. Tita Gray

The main point of this concept is to educate you from the outside (Industries) so that you can make informed decisions between what you are learning in the classroom and how it correlates to a fulfilling career. Isn't the whole point of education the outcome? No one has a crystal ball to determine their career destination; however, you do have the power and ability to control your journey toward a rewarding career. The 3 Circle Concept begins as follows:

1. The outer circle illustrates the vast number of industries to choose from. If you are not certain about which career field you prefer, select three and conduct research. Chapter Eight has an extensive list of industries you might consider.

2. The middle circle describes companies. I recommend you think about what type of work you'd like to do and review several companies within your industry of interest. It's also important to think about whether you want to be local or expand your horizons in another state or globally. For example, when I thought about pursuing a career in education and being a teacher, I knew I only wanted to teach in a college setting. I also knew that for personal reasons, I wanted to relocate to San Diego. After coming to that realization, I began researching every four-year and two-year college/university in that geographical area.

3. The inner circle represents jobs. This is the fun part and where your major begins to make more sense. Once you select the companies you'd be interested in working for, it's time to start researching job descriptions. For example, an entry level public relations position might be described like this:

Responsibilities:

- *Managing and executing projects as assigned by the Marketing Manager*
- *Working with the Marketing Manager and key accounts to integrate PR campaigns with customer promotions*
- *Coordinating in-store service events and maintaining successful operation*
- *Building relationships with customers and communicating promotional services*
- *Working with the Marketing Manager to develop and refine measurement strategies for PR campaigns*
- *Development of promotional marketing materials and visual merchandising*
- *Developing and maintaining relationships with suppliers and retail event personnel*
- *Keeping accurate and timely records of event traffic, production, and inventory*
- *Identifying new opportunities and efficiency innovations*
- *Position will be considered for senior campaign management roles based on performance*

Position's Requirements:

- *1-2 years' experience in marketing, sales or communications OR internship in related field*
- *Excellent written and verbal communication skills*
- *Ability to work in a fast-paced environment and deliver results while managing multiple projects*
- *Level headed problem solver with a professional service oriented attitude*
- *Superb organizational and tracking skills with great attention to detail*
- *Team player who also excels as an individual contributor*
- *Adaptable, dependable and responsible*
- *Basic understanding of marketing concepts and sales strategy*
- *Proficient in Microsoft Office*
- *Position will be considered for senior campaign management roles*

A job description for a financial analyst may look like this:

Responsibilities:

- *Prepare financial analyses and assist in development of financial forecasts and closings*
- *Collect financial data and ensure conformity with corporate policies and procedures*
- *Prepare operations reports for presentation to management*
- *Analyze operational financial data, investigate variances and investigate their impact on planned objectives*
- *Perform budget analysis, and cash flow analysis*
- *Provide analytical support to senior management; identify trends and recommend changes to reduce company costs*

Required Experience

- *Bachelor's Degree in Finance or Accounting*
- *0-2 years related of work experience*
- *Strong Excel is a must (pivot tables-Lookups) and PowerPoint*
- *Bilingual in Spanish is a must*
- *Attention to detail and accuracy are extremely critical*
- *Excellent communication and interpersonal skills*

Once you have reviewed several job descriptions you can begin matching or comparing the skill sets needed in that job with the major you are interested in studying. As you can see in the financial analyst example, speaking Spanish is a must, particularly for this company's geographical area. Also, knowing how to perform budget and cash flow analyses is a needed skill set. I will discuss selecting a major in more depth in Chapter Three.

Student Story

Anthony was a student in both my Organizational Behavior and Leadership in Organizations classes. He came to me one day before class began and asked to speak to me. He seemed very unsettled. He stated that his family wanted him to pursue a career in medicine; however, he was very interested in being a personal trainer. To his family, being a personal trainer was not reputable and probably had no monetary value. For him, it was a meaningful and fulfilling way to help people stay healthy and alleviate the need for medical attention.

I suggested he get an internship in a hospital and see if he felt a connection to the work and industry. We both agreed he could always pursue being a personal trainer at a later time in life. Time went by and Anthony shared an incident that happened while he was interning at a hospital and it solidified his decision that he didn't want to pursue medicine. He graduated and moved forward with his passion of becoming a personal trainer and although he has had to work hard, four years later he has a successful practice and finds the time to travel around the world for fun. (By the way, I was one of his first clients.)

Summary

Students: Please take the time to research the vast opportunities that are out there for you. Look at big, medium, and small companies. Start researching a few industries and make a list of all of the different types of jobs available in the companies you are researching. Also, pay attention to the culture of the industry. I talk more about this in Chapter Five.

Families/Friends: Share your stories of career preparation, or lack thereof, and how it has impacted where you are today. Try not to encourage your student to do something that's just for money and, instead, encourage them to critically think about their strengths and weaknesses. It's okay for them to enter college undecided on a major and take a year to discover and research themselves and what career path is true to who they are.

Two

Career Preparation
What is it?

"The best preparation for tomorrow is doing your best today."
— H. Jackson Browne Jr.

"Smart people learn from their own mistakes and wise people learn from the mistakes from others." — Unknown

Let me begin by saying: a major does *not* equate to a career. It's only one aspect to preparing you for a job. It's a competitive tool and a way to demonstrate that you have transferable knowledge. Let me emphasize that a classroom education provides you with transferable knowledge, not necessarily transferable skills, unless there is hands-on learning. Students must have internships, conduct research, shadow professionals, and other forms of experiential learning to gain skills. As I've said, a job does not equate to a career. A major and a job are part of the preparation for a career.

Due to a lack of targeted and informed career preparation, it takes the average college graduate up to six months to secure employment after graduation. Therefore, what is most needed are career strategies that begin when starting college. A survey completed by employers suggested that students are prepared for and anticipate their first job, but not for careers that require critical thinking, self-direction, and management of uncertainty (Peter D. Hart Research Associates, 2008). In *Learning Reconsidered: A Campus-Wide Focus on the Student Experience*, Keeling (2004) suggested that universities and colleges must clarify their role in educating students in a way that will assist them not only during their time as students, but in the important life choices they will make in the future. As a result, cognitive complexity, interpersonal and intrapersonal competence, civic engagement, and humanitarianism are among the desirable learning outcomes for students.

The expectations of higher education today include wide-ranging goals of soft skills and outcomes such as mature decision-making, intrapersonal adeptness, appreciation of diverse perspectives, interpersonal relationships with others, and critical thinking. As future employees, individuals need to demonstrate having transferable skills. In other words, skills acquired through school, work, and personal experiences.

Transferable skills vary. They can include active listening, critical thinking, decision making, leading others, and problem solving. These are some of the skills that intersect jobs, companies, and industries. Opportunities to obtain these skills are available on campuses nationally. However, many college seniors believe that four or more years of college haven't adequately prepared them to begin work after graduation. And like these students, many of you may still have a difficult time seeing how the skills you are learning or learned in college will transfer to the workplace. Let's discuss this further.

Planning

Planning for a career should begin when you are freshmen, if not before, and can be the catalyst for your choice of majors. Unfortunately, many of you are choosing your majors because of family or friends' influence before having a thorough understanding of yourself and your career goals. Constructing a career goal is an important aspect of college and an individual's maturity, with the selection of a major as a formal step in this process. However, major selection should not be the first step. The impact of choosing a major has consequences lasting way beyond a student's learning and satisfaction.

Career planning should begin with self-awareness, self-knowledge, awareness of industries and the companies within those industries, jobs within those companies, and then you will have a better idea of how to choose a major. Universities could benefit greatly by providing workshops, mentoring, and classes for students while they are in their freshman and sophomore years regarding knowledge and impacts of U.S. and global industries. Inevitably, students will view their path as career related and that it will assist them in choosing a major that will correlate with their industry of interest.

Planning Steps

Take time to understand yourself. If you are in the younger years of your life, begin to focus on what brings you joy. I'm not talking about the joy you find in partying (LOL). I mean your dreams and thoughts of where you see yourself in the future. What are your likes and dislikes? If you are more mature and have already experienced life through the lens of an adult with responsibilities, take time to assess who you are and who you would like to become. Understand that it is never too late to transition into your dream career. I highly encourage you to take every self-assessment available (a list is provided in Chapter Three) and incorporate self-reflection, journaling, and/or developing a mind map.

1. Get information about transferable skills that peak your interest in a certain field. I suggest you check out Massive Open Online Courses (MOOCs). MOOCs are available for anyone to enroll and provide a flexible and affordable way to learn new skills, advance your career, and deliver quality educational experiences. The MOOC that I suggest is through coursera.org. You can check out a course or pursue a certification for free or for almost nothing. A list of MOOCs is provided in Chapter Seven.

2. Once you have a better idea of what you want to have more knowledge about, begin investigating or researching industries that you have always been interested in working for (see Chapter Five for an industry list). In addition, set up a LinkedIn account and begin adding as many professional contacts as possible. You can also use LinkedIn as a way of informally reaching out to people in the industries you're interested in.

3. Next, look into internships, volunteering, or conducting informal interviews with people in your field of interest. Make doing this a full-time job. Tell everyone you know exactly what type of work you are interested in and for what companies. Review companies through Glassdoor to see what former and current employees are saying. Look at job descriptions to make sure the qualifications match up with the major you are considering or have selected.

4. Tailor your resume to your strengths, meaning include numbers, percentages, and results. It should be written so that it summarizes stories about your journey. Your resume should be the key to how your interview aligns with your experience. When you are in an interview, answer questions based on the STAR model

- Situation, Task, Action, and Result. Most employers rate your answers based on this or a similar model. For students that have not had full-time employment yet, now is the time to start looking for internships, volunteer opportunities, and part-time gigs.

5. Create SMART Goals for every aspect of your planning. SMART stands for Specific, Measurable, Attainable, Realistic, and Timeframe. Why is this extremely important? SMART goals keep you accountable to yourself! It touches on each detail and implementation of your goal attainment.

6. Create a Mind Map, which is a visual processing tool that helps you structure your thoughts and information so that you can better analyze, comprehend, synthesize, recall and generate new ideas. Below is an example of a mind map.

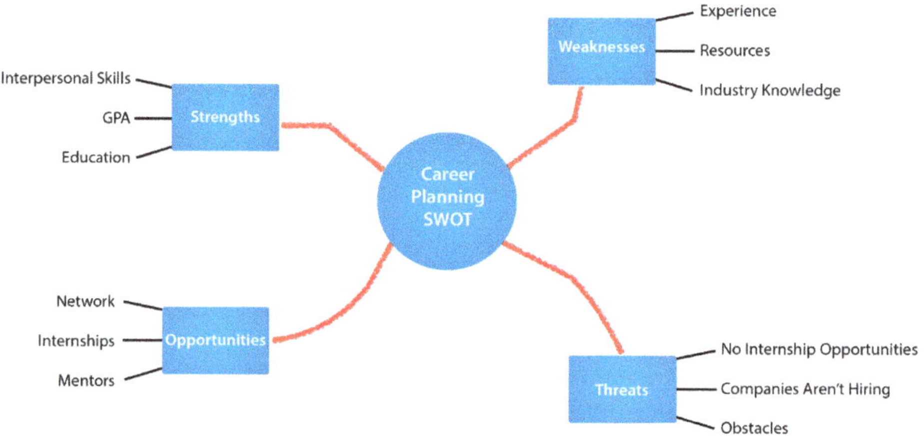

Transition

Deciding on a career is an important aspect of transitioning from adolescent roles to joining the adult workforce. Planning your transition from college into the workforce is a life-changing phenomenon. As you begin to research industries, companies, jobs, and majors, when it comes time to make a choice you might consider relocating. As you are preparing for change it's important to understand that change is not always easy, yet it can be one of the most rewarding things you'll ever do for your career.

One of the most profound theories that I ever researched was that of transition theory developed 35 years ago by a woman named Nancy Schlossberg. She developed this theory based on her experience transitioning to a new job in another state, which she assumed would've been easy, but came with unexplained confusion and stress. Schlossberg identified three aspects to transition: anticipated, unanticipated, and nonevent. An anticipated transition is major life event that we expect to happen, such as graduating, starting a new job, or changing careers. Unanticipated transitions are disruptive events that occur unexpectedly, such as a bad accident, severe illness, or a surprise promotion. Nonevents are expected events that fail, such as not graduating, not getting a job upon graduation, or not getting a promotion. The three transition events are significant because preparing for change is just as salient as the change itself and without being self-aware, your ability to adapt could be very good or very bad.

As you transition through college, every year will bring new developments, some good and maybe some bad. Always keep in mind that you are on a journey and the destination, no matter how well we prepare, is not guaranteed. Start preparing yourself physically and emotionally for transition—it will be a game changer.

Student Story

Alexis was a focused and determined student. She was a business major with a marketing concentration focused on sports. She worked for San Diego State University's athletic department. She always knew that she wanted to work in the sports industry and she stayed diligent in her pursuit, making serious sacrifices at times. She was growing in awareness of her strengths and weaknesses, took the time for self-reflection, and constantly sought out guidance from people whom she trusted (360 degree feedback) and I was lucky enough to be one of them. She always believed her purpose was to serve professional athletes in a meaningful way based on their health, wellness, and contribution to the sport. Since she had been a student athlete, she had knowledge about the personal aspect of being an athlete and the sacrifices and challenges that they face. What she wanted to gain from her major was the management skills needed to be a top-notch executive. Outside the classroom, Alexis attended leadership events, created SMART goals, and mapped out the direction she wanted for her career journey. Although she faced disappointment, she was passionate about staying the course.

Alexis would meet with me, call me, or text me about the highs and lows she was experiencing in pursuit of a chance to work in the professional sports industry. She accepted sports internships that were either for minimal or no pay. At times she faced sexist behavior from men in the industry, which provided her with awareness of the industry's frequent culture (I discuss culture in Chapter Six). There were times when she was not called back for an interview, although she was lead to believe that she did well. The disappointment in her voice always made me sad, but I reassured her it was their loss and something better was coming—just hang in there. I told her that you only fail when you stop trying and that the disappointments make you stronger.

One day I received a text from Alexis saying that a potential employer would be reaching out to me since I was listed as a referral. When I got the call, I spoke about Alexis' purpose, passion, knowledge, and personal connection to the sports industry. At that moment, the employer said, "I shouldn't say this, but we are going to hire her and your assessment of her is exactly what we wanted to hear." Alexis aligned her major with the knowledge and skills to master her dream job and was preparing for the transition.

Summary

Students: Please take the time to become aware of what you want out of life. Career planning should begin with the resources that are around you, family, mentors, and campus career services. Take every assessment possible. Make sure that the major you choose is aligned with head, heart, and mind. When mind, body, and soul are not aligned with something you will be devoting a considerable amount of money, time, and energy towards, you will feel a disconnect. Always take the time to create SMART goals and plan out your thoughts.

Families/Friends: Encourage your student to look beyond the obvious. For example, not every person good at sports will become a professional athlete—actually the percentage is around 5%. However, they can find other types of contributions to that industry. Help them to think about the big picture. For those of you who went to college, how many of you are working in the field of your undergraduate major? Probably not many, so share your story of why you chose your major, what shaped your decisions, and if you have had a fulfilling career. Share what you did to prepare for your career or what you wish you had done in hindsight.

Three

Choosing a Major
How it begins

"Never give up on what you really want to do. The person with big dreams is more powerful than the one with all the facts."
— *H. Jackson Brown, Jr.*

Plain and simple, your major is your specialized area of study. It's the area in which you strive to become a subject matter expert in a field that will provide you with a successful career, right? Isn't that the whole point of college...the outcome? Unfortunately, the major that you choose will not predict nor promise your future. Most graduates find jobs that have nothing to do with what they studied as an undergrad. I remember attending a conference and in one of the larger workshops (probably 300 people), the facilitator asked how many of us were working in the field that we studied as undergrads. Only three people raised their hands. It was astonishing, yet customary. According to the U.S. Bureau of Labor Statistics the average person in their 20's switches jobs once every three years and the average person can change careers three or more times in their lifetime. A survey conducted by Strada Education Network and Gallup of 32,000 students from 42 randomly selected four-year institutions showed that only 53% of students believe their major will lead to a good job.

So how do you prepare to choose the correct major or at least the field of study that will bring you prosperity, happiness, and opportunity? It begins with self-awareness. The first thing I suggest all students do as soon as they are preparing for college or while in college, is to complete as many self-assessment tools as possible. Begin the process immediately to better understand your personal likes and dislikes. For example, are you an introvert or extravert, do you like fast-paced environments, do you enjoy writing, are you very analytical, and is your learning style visual, aural, verbal or physical? A lack of such knowledge about yourself can be devastating to your learning processes and outcomes. The self-awareness process can provide you with greater control over events in your life, particularly like the college-to-workforce transition.

I was told by a researcher that we spend 70% of our lives working, so doing what you love is critical. Take time to visualize and dream of where you see yourself in the future. Do you see yourself around people who need medical attention, do you see yourself in an office, do you visualize yourself interacting with people globally, do you see yourself working with animals or working outside with your hands, do you see yourself protecting the environment or lobbying for a cause you believe in? What's inside of you that feeds your soul when you think about it? It's imperative that you spend time working on your self-awareness and self-actualization and then begin the process of asking yourself…is this the right major? When you have a chance, check out the Scott Dinsmore *TED Talk* recorded in 2012. He discusses pursuing something that you cannot live without doing. He talks about finding your purpose. It's an amazing TED Talk. Dinsmore, hiking with his wife in 2015, tragically died doing what he loved, something he preached through his work.

Picking a major should be done once you have researched your industry and taken several personal/career assessments. Once you've completed those tasks, begin to look at internships, mentors, and informal interviews with people who are working in your fields of interest. Go to your school's career services department and inquire about internships. If you're receiving financial aid, apply for work study in a department that you're interested in. For example, if you really love sports and might want a career in that industry, see if you can work in athletics, particularly if the school is Division I or II. If you're interested in finance, inquire about student assistant jobs in the operations or foundation departments. Check out the University of California Berkeley Career Center to see how areas of a major corresponds to industries. Also, review PayScale's 2017-2018 College Salary Report which ranks undergraduate and 2-year colleges by the highest earning graduates.

Remember, your major is there to give you transferable knowledge. You mainly earn skills by doing them. So get out there and just do it!

Student Story

Celeste was an accounting major and a senior. I knew her well as a smart, engaged, and academically focused student. One day she came to see me because she realized that she didn't want to be an accountant and, since she was about to graduate, this realization was extremely upsetting. She stated very emphatically that she didn't want to sit behind a desk running numbers; instead, she wanted to do something that would give back to others. I lovingly reassured her that the skills she's learned in accounting could be applied in any industry. So I asked, "What industry are you interested in working in?" She had no idea, but stressed wanting to work with people and make a difference. As a result, I suggested philanthropy. She wasn't aware of the philanthropic industry, so I explained that philanthropists give back to communities and, since the non-profit companies applying for funding have to include financial statements, accountants were always needed on either side of the equation. Mainly we discussed how her major provided transferable knowledge that could apply in many different industries. The emphasis was on finding herself, her purpose, and her passion. I don't know if she decided to pursue a career in philanthropy, but after sharing the 3CC I know that the conversation left her feeling much more empowered regarding how to intertwine her major into career planning.

Summary

Students: If you do not enjoy math or science, why are you pursing a major that requires it? For example, if your heart and soul are into dance, why not research every aspect of that field? Even if you are not the greatest dancer, you could be a choreographer, teacher, or open a dance studio and provide opportunities for others. Having a clear understanding of your values is a critical step to knowing what you stand for.

Families/Friends: Discuss your student's major and how they selected it. (If you didn't go to college, recommend they talk to someone who did.) What was the basis of your decision on a major? Why was it fulfilling or not? Instead of telling your student what you believe they should major in, encourage them to research their interest. Do not guide them to careers that have false promises of monetary gain. People make the most out of their careers when they do what they love.

Four

Self-Awareness

Purpose, passion, knowledge, personal

"Knowing others is intelligence; knowing yourself is true wisdom. Mastering others is strength; mastering yourself is true power."
— *Lao-Tsu*

Becoming self-aware is a journey, not a destination. It takes patience, constant evaluation, and reflection. To deal with the forms of stress and overall life changes created by the onset of maturity, you must have a strong grasp of your own emotional well-being. Emotional well-being can be defined as one's ability to feel comfortable with self, relate to others, handle disappointments, solve problems, celebrate successes, and critically think (Page & Page, 1992). Students generally do not anticipate the emotional stress and the changes they will experience in developing themselves to be professionals. The likelihood is that you can't comprehend what being a professional is like, yet you know that you are going to become one.

I would like to dissect the definition of self-awareness. If awareness is the ability to know, feel or perceive, then self-awareness is the ability to know, feel, or perceive things about yourself. As a society, the usual way in which we gain understanding of ourselves is through experiences and our reactions to those experiences. Although trial and error play a natural part of human evolution, you should be more purposeful in advancing your self-awareness.

I highly encourage you to take career self-assessments right before you embark on a new career path, including college. While working at SDSU through a grant I was awarded, I developed an app that was based on Holland's Six Personality Types primarily so that students could have a better understanding of how their personalities match up with career choices and majors. While conducting research for the grant I found that many students were in majors that did not match up to their personality. When you utilize self-assessments you will begin the habit of self-reflection and, inevitably, finding your purpose and passion. There are many career self-assessments available including:

- 360 Degree Feedback: A feedback process where your friends, family, and/or mentors evaluate you. You receive an analysis of how you perceive yourself and how others perceive you.

- Holland's Six Personality Types: An assessment based on the theory that if people are aware of their personality type or combination of types—realistic, investigative, artistic, social, enterprising or conventional—then they will be happier workers.

- Myers-Briggs Type Indicator: MBTI is an introspective self-report questionnaire with the purpose of indicating differing psychological preferences in how people perceive the world around them and make decisions.

- Strengths Finder: A self-help book. At the heart of the book is the Internet-based "Clifton Strengths Finder," an online personal assessment test that profiles the user's strengths. The authors advocate focusing on building strengths rather than focusing on weaknesses.

- True Colors Personality Test: A people technology that uses four colors (orange, gold, green, and blue) to represent each of the temperament/personality types. It can help increase understanding of yourself and others as well as improve communication.

- Keirsey Temperament Sorter: The KTS is a self-assessed personality questionnaire designed to help people better understand themselves and others. It's one of the most widely used personality assessments in the world.

- Big Five Personality Test: Identifies five broad domains that define human personality and account for individual differences. This test is an overarching assessment of your personality, which will provide you with a much richer understanding of who you are as a person.

- MAPP Test: The first and most comprehensive career test online. More than 8 million people in nearly every country in the world have taken the MAPP test.

Use these assessments as a barometer of where you are today. If you disagree with the results of an assessment, remember that you selected the choices. Take time to reflect on the results instead of judging them—you just might find that who you *think* you are is in conflict with who you *really* are. As a matter of fact, there is an excellent book, a classic called *Do What You Are*, that I highly recommend. This book is probably my favorite of all career preparation books because the authors emphasize concentrating on who you are and the rest falls into place. According to the authors, when you are in the most fulfilling job, you should:

- Look forward to going to work

- Feel energized (most of the time) by what you do

- Feel your contribution is respected and appreciated

- Feel proud when describing your work to others

- Enjoy and respect the people you work with

- Feel optimistic about your future

Knowing who you are is the most critical and vital aspect to career satisfaction. Let me give you an example. If most of your life you thought about being an educator and then took several career assessments for personality type and they all come back saying that you would be good at teaching, good at math or science, like giving back, and very analytical, you might pursue teaching, right? If you are self-aware you will know that, although you want to teach, you only want to teach college students, not elementary kids. In other words, knowing the type of work that you want to do is one piece of the puzzle. However, it is imperative that you are aware of the environment and setting in which you want to do the work.

Purpose

At this point in your journey you might not know your life's purpose, which is fine, because more profoundly, it's knowing your purpose in life that's paramount. Your life will always be evolving and it will change more times than you will be able to count. However, as you prepare for your career aspirations, being aware of your purpose is critical. So how do you find your purpose? By doing, learning, researching, feeling, talking, loving, reading, traveling, exploring, dreaming, writing, taking chances—all with the intent of knowing what excites you and what doesn't.

You find your purpose by doing things and reflecting on how those things have impacted you. Pay attention to the things that create an emotional reaction within you, whether you like the feeling or not. Also, do not limit yourself to just one thing. You will find many things that interest you, so explore all of them in some way. For example, I love writing, I love public speaking, I love teaching, I love strategic thinking, I love life and career coaching, and I love exercising. Everything I listed relates in some way to my purpose in life, which is giving back to college students. Your purpose will infuse your passion. Find your passion and go after it like your life depends on it, because it does.

Passion

I had a serious "aha" moment as I was reading *Leadership in the Crucible of Work* for one of my doctorate classes and the author mentioned that the word "passion" is vastly misunderstood. He stated that most people believe passion is defined as something that you feel very strongly about, or something you want badly, but he said we're mistaken. He stated that passion is defined by what you are willing to sacrifice. Defining passion as what you're willing to sacrifice was most profound for me because I have always used passion as one of my values. Knowing that the root of the word passion comes from the Latin word *passire*, meaning to suffer, as in the unfathomable sacrifice of suffering in the Passion of Christ, brought a whole new meaning to the word. At that point I understood the connection; knowing your passion in life gives you a sense of purpose. It's what you're willing to sacrifice having less of, including sleep, love, food, travel, or money. Take the time to find your passion because where, how, and what you find may surprise you.

I made a decision to leave corporate America to pursue a career in academia. In an effort to stay on course in my new career, I pursued a doctorate degree. I sacrificed seeing my family, friends, going to events, and traveling in an effort to finish my degree because I was passionate about why I was doing it. When I reflect, all of my sacrifices were fruitful and made me who I have become and allowed me to do what I love. You will persist when you believe in what you're doing more than you want to breathe, as my friend Dr. Eric Thomas will attest.

As you reflect on your passion, think of what it is in life that you cannot do without. Your passion for something may be a hobby—you cannot go without working out, writing poetry, creating new music, or some other art form, traveling, etc. Bill Gates and Steve Jobs sacrificed finishing college to pursue their passion and although I am not encouraging anyone to drop out of school, I do want you to find something in life that you need or believe in so badly that you'll make sacrifices for it.

Knowledge

Knowledge is defined as awareness or familiarity gained by experience of a fact or situation. Knowledge is your key to greatness. The ways of the world are at your fingertips. Before college or while in college you have the ability to take online MOOC courses, earn certificates, or take a class regarding something that you're interested in and you can do it in your freshman year to make sure you are selecting the correct major.

Why the hell do you begin a major that you have no knowledge about? C'mon man! Why waste your time, money, and energy pursuing anything that you are not knowledgeable about. I am not talking about what your family, friends, and professors know about—I mean what YOU are knowledgeable of. The more that you know about what you want to pursue as a career, the more power you are giving yourself to make the best decisions. Yes, knowledge is power. Knowledge is impressionable, influential, and a game changer.

When looking at career knowledge, think about the industry, companies, and jobs within a trade and ask yourself, will you enjoy these duties, tasks, and responsibilities? Will you be proud of the work you do on a daily basis? Do you get to be creative or is it more routine? Would you find it challenging and rewarding? Does the work fit into your long-term career objectives? Will it offer a variety of work assignments? How much autonomy will you have? Is the nature of the work more project oriented? Will you be working with people, ideas, data, or things? Can you balance the duties with your other commitments? Does the work involve intangibles or concrete and observable outcomes? Does it require leadership skills or can you be more of an independent contributor? What's the workload?

The most import thing to remember is that you are what you do, so finding something purposeful is critical to personal satisfaction.

Personal

> *"Leaders must continually ask: is my work worthy of my sense of purpose, or just a means to an end?" — Sandy Shugart PhD*

You should strive to have a deep and personal connection to the work that you'll do day after day. When you have a personal connection, you bring your best to work every day. Your happiness, confidence, and influence will increase regularly whether you are going through good times or bad. You will care about the people you work with in a meaningful manner. Throughout your career, particularly in your industry, your reputation will precede you as someone who is knowledgeable and committed to their work.

I strongly suggest that your personal alignment begin with knowing your top five values. I remember giving a values exercise in my leadership class and a student told me that he spent three frustrating hours trying to narrow down his top five values. My question to him was, "When was the last time that you spent three hours devoted to knowing yourself?" He said, "Never!" Many of my students did not think that this lesson was important until they were interviewing. I learned this lesson the hard way.

Years ago when I was working in the music industry, I had an interview for an important position at a major record label. I was very prepared for and confident about the interview. Upon meeting with the vice president, she told me that my recommendations were solid, my resume was excellent, and that I probably knew a lot about the company. As a result, she began the interview by asking me to tell her a little about myself. No problem! Next, she asked, "What are your top five values?" I remember like it was yesterday; the sinking feeling that I had as I was trying hard to come up with a truthful answer... and it was written all over my face. I thought to myself, be honest, so I smiled and said "I have never thought about this and would you mind if I called you tomorrow with the answer after I put intentional thought to it?" She said yes and resumed the interview. Although I answered the rest of the interview questions well, I could not get past not knowing the values question. I felt stupid for not knowing the answer—it was about me! I called her the next morning and gave my values. She thanked me and said that knowing my values were important because they would be a significant aspect of what I brought to work every day. She spoke of the importance of my values being in line with the values of the organization at which I chose to work. It was one of the most important lessons I ever learned about myself. I share it constantly so that others will not be unprepared.

You must have a personal connection to who you are and what in life is most meaningful to you today. Your values will change over time as your priorities in life change, but wherever you are in your journey, be intentional about your values. Your values must align with your purpose, passion, knowledge, and personal.

Student Story

Tim was a student of mine with a smile and sense of humor that brightened every class. I enjoyed his inquisitiveness and joy of life. Even when the class ended, he would often email me about his career plans and we would discuss different companies at length. I had become a mentor and someone whom he relied upon for advice. I recall one day while working on an important project hearing a discussion taking place outside of my office. It was Tim, asking my assistant if he could speak to me for just a minute. I could hear the urgency in his voice so I called out to him to come in. He graciously apologized for the intrusion. Although I was concerned, he was smiling, and began to tell me a story that he could barely contain. He said that he just attended a career fair and upon meeting with an employer, they asked about his top values. He could not believe that exactly what I shared in class happened to him and it made his awareness of self so much more relevant. He was so happy that he had been prepared with an answer and appreciative that I shared my story.

I remember receiving emails and calls from Tim up to a year after he graduated. He still had not landed his dream job. All that I could do was make sure that he was prepared; I knew it was coming. One day he called, telling me about landing an awesome position with an amazing Fortune 500 company. He felt self-aware, understood his purpose, was knowledgeable about the industry, and had a personal commitment to what he was going to do. He demonstrated passion by never giving up or just settling for less. He is currently on a fast track to becoming a manager. He even recommended and afforded me the opportunity to speak to the company's senior officers for one of their managers' meetings and I think I made him proud.

Summary

Students: I want to reiterate: knowing thyself is the most important aspect to a healthy, happy, and fulfilling career. Many people are great at interviews and can say all the right things about how knowledgeable they are regarding the position. It's when employers begin digging deeper into your knowledge about who you are that the disconnect becomes apparent. Being authentic is easy when you are true to yourself. Having a clear understanding of your values is a critical step to knowing what you stand for.

Families/Friends: Share your stories of career preparation or lack thereof and how it has impacted where you are today. Try not to encourage your student to do something that is best for you and instead encourage them to critically think about their strengths and weaknesses. Talk about your journey to self-awareness or lack thereof. It's okay for you to not have all of the answers, but you must encourage your loved ones to find their own.

Five

Industry Choice

Building a career

"Your work is going to fill a large part of your life, and the only way to be truly satisfied is to do what you believe is great work. And the only way to do great work is to love what you do. If you haven't found it yet, keep looking. Don't settle. As with all matters of the heart, you'll know when you find it." — Steve Jobs

You will spend a large part your adult life at work and it can significantly affect your well-being. This is why choosing a career is something that you shouldn't take lightly. It's important to examine all of the options available to you before you make a final decision as this will help ensure your future professional happiness and security.

Determining the right industry helps you zero in on the ideal career, which minimizes the risk of making a wrong decision. By looking at the industries, rather than individual professions, you can identify the fastest growing industries that can help you find a job more easily, while it can also help you choose a career based on how lucrative a field is expected to be. According to a forecast from the Institute for the Future (IFTF), 85% of the jobs in 2030 haven't even been invented yet. Ten years after that, the workforce may be totally unrecognizable.

Making the Choice

So how do you choose the right industry?

- I suggest that you think about all of the things that you like or that intrigue you. Automation will be a huge trend in the coming years. Do you love teaching, guiding, influencing others? Do you love cars and everything about automobiles? Are you intrigued by the stock and financial markets? Do you want to start a business in a particular industry?

- Is your motivation to make a difference in the world? Do you want to make a difference in health care? Do you want to make a difference in how animals are treated? Do you want to change labor laws or human trafficking?

- Think like an entrepreneur! If you were going to start a business you'd probably research the market thoroughly, understand the product or service in depth, and have an understanding of staffing needs. This is how you should proceed in knowing your industry. When you approach knowing your industry in this manner, you will excel in almost any interview.

Although it's critical to know your purpose, passion, knowledge, and personal connection, it is just as important to be informed about every aspect of the industry that you're interested in. Once you have an idea of at least two industries that spark your curiosity, next you must gain hands-on experience.

Gaining Experience

There is nothing more important than gaining hands-on experience. Aristotle wrote, "For the things we have to learn before we can do them, we learn by doing them." Studies have found that students would rather engage in kinesthetic (hands-on) learning than listen to a lecture. It provides you with a way of learning from your mistakes and seeing how practice and theory work in tandem. There is really no better way to gain experience than through an internship.

I remember a marketing student complaining about how she had a sales internship and hated the work. In an effort to have a discussion on career planning, I asked her what she didn't like and why. She said that she didn't like sitting at a desk all day making sales calls, that it was boring. I asked her what she would like to be doing. She said she'd prefer face-to-face interaction that included some analytical reporting. I also inquired about the industry of her internship and she said that she never researched it, but assumed it wouldn't be something of interest in the future. I explained that the internship was probably one of the best things that could have happened to her because it demonstrated what she *does not want to do,* which is just as important as what she *does want to do.*

Student Story

Aleksey was one of my organizational behavior students. He didn't like college very much, but he was committed to graduating because of a promise he made to his mom. His mom passed away from cancer while he was a student and when I met him, he was trying hard just to manage life. Although he wasn't terribly interested in the class, he was intrigued by my background in the music industry. Our mutual enthusiasm regarding music created a lasting bond that went from student and teacher to Godson and Godmother.

Aleksey knew at a young age that he wanted to be a music producer. He loved Hip Hop and R&B and was passionate about becoming successful in the industry. Although upon graduating he knew and still knows that he has to maintain some kind of income, he has always put his work in music first. He is sacrificing everything to establish a career in music. For him it is his joy, purpose, passion, knowledge, and personal. He has shared that the thought of not pursuing his career makes him depressed. I know that he will be successful in life because he is doing what brings him happiness and fulfillment and although he might not be making monetary gains yet, he is following his dreams.

Summary

Students: Doing what you love can mean sacrificing a big salary, or having acceptance from your family, or being able to go on trips with your friends. It can require working more hours and having sleepless nights. However, there is no greater feeling than loving what you do and feeling pride in what you spend 8 to 10 hours a day doing. Even if you have to take a job just to pay the bills, never stop seeking the career in an industry that you want to grow in. See and seize your future!

Families/Friends: Please encourage your loved one to follow their dream. Let them know that you will be there through the good and bad times. By pushing them toward greatness in what fulfills their purpose, you are pushing them towards a future of less uncertainty and doubt. It doesn't mean that every job will be ideal—that's life—but it will mean that their choices with be more meaningful.

Six

Culture Fit

What it is, how to identify it, how to align yourself

Culture Defined

Culture is the implicit environment of an organization. Culture influences behaviors, norms, and attitudes within an organization. Cultural norms stipulate what is encouraged, discouraged, accepted, or rejected within different areas in an organization. Culture is developed through such things as the combined experiences, values, and assumptions held by employees. A company's culture can be understood by observing the behaviors of its leaders and employees. Don't take culture for granted!

Culture Identified

Cultural themes come in many layers. As you are researching industries, keep in mind that each industry has its own implicit culture. For example, the finance, technology, and education industries all have very different cultural norms. Many of these norms have been passed down for centuries and many of them are new. Millennial entrepreneurs, successful or not, usually start companies with cultures based on flexible schedules, creativity, laid-back dress codes, collaboration, and are highly motivated by purpose. It is imperative that you ask companies you interview with about the company culture, particularly in the department that you will be assigned to.

Examples of culture elements are:

- How are new ideas received?
- What amenities are available for employees?
- How is information communicated?
- Do the leaders lead by example?
- How are new employees viewed?
- How are mistakes perceived?
- What information is shared and with whom?
- How do teams interact with one another?
- How are customers treated?
- What behaviors get you promoted?

Culture Alignment

Once your self-awareness is strong and you know your values, likes, and dislikes, then you will be more knowledgeable about the culture fit that is right for you. It's very important for you to gain an understanding of the culture of your industry of choice. Furthermore, it's just as critical that you are aware of the culture of the companies that you are interested in working for. I cannot emphasize how important it is to find out as much as possible about the culture of the companies that you interview with.

There are thousands of companies that have great reputations externally yet, unfortunately, it's not until you work for them or a specific department that you see the true attitudes and behaviors. When your personal values, drives, and needs are properly aligned with your work environment, culture can unleash enormous amounts of energy toward a shared purpose, meaning, and successful career. Check out the following videos of companies and their culture:

- Google: http://www.youtube.com/watch?v=aOZhbOhEunY
- Zappos: https://www.youtube.com/watch?v=tFyW5s_7ZWc

- Hubspot: https://www.youtube.com/watch?time_continue=35&v=EXOtTvb5OFE

- Starbucks: https://www.youtube.com/watch?v=xnHeuoaK3Eg

- KPMG: https://www.youtube.com/watch?v=yBJLI2kN8vY

- Kaiser Permanente: https://www.youtube.com/watch?v=W8cuhK_jZH4

My Story

I had the pleasure of working for an amazing utility for eight years. I had not worked for a utility previously and had no knowledge of the culture, but had the skills needed to do the particular job that was posted. I remember it like it was yesterday; how awkward I felt when I began working there. The average age was 45, almost 75% were white males, the average time of employment was 28 years, and it was very conservative. My first supervisor was not comfortable with African Americans. I realized almost immediately that I was hired because the role (supplier diversity) required meeting, negotiating, and advocating for minority businesses so it was perfect for an African American. Although getting acclimated to working at the utility was difficult, I enjoyed the work I did and some of my colleagues are still close friends to this day.

As stated, culture is the implicit environment of an organization. When there is a good culture fit, you love what you do and are excited to come into work every morning. You want to see the company grow and actively contribute to that growth. Although I cared for most of my colleagues and made a great salary, I never quite felt a fit in the culture. I did see value in the work I did, but never felt a sense of purpose or passion about growing in the company. Basically, I didn't feel a strong connection to the utility industry. Once I came to terms with my purpose, I pursued a career in education and it has been one of the best decisions I ever made in my life.

Summary

Students: There will be a time when you will be dissatisfied with your job because of the culture and, inadvertently, the people you work with. Unfortunately, most times there isn't anything you can do about it once you're in it. I know this firsthand. Use resources like LinkedIn and Glassdoor to gauge the environment before you interview with a company. Ask questions about the personnel demographics of the company, ask about how they hire and fire people, and ask about how promotions are given. Pay strong attention to the hierarchical structure of the company.

Families/Friends: Students are going to work in places that they love and that they hate. Give them advice on what to do when they are not happy. Share your experience on power dynamics and leadership. The more knowledge and information they have before graduating, the better prepared that they will be at handling adversity—which is why having internships is so invaluable.

Seven

Resources

Skills needed to be on your game!

"An obstacle is something you see when you take your eyes off of your goal." — Unknown

The U.S. Bureau of Labor Statistics (https://www.bls.gov/audience/ jobseekers.htm) provides a variety of useful reports on employment statistics and 10-year forecasts. Check them out to establish if the career you've chosen is experiencing, or is likely to experience, a talent shortage. If so, you can expect a higher starting salary or more appealing perks if your skills match up with employers' needs. Test your work-related skill set at Mind Tools (https://www.mindtools. com) to find out how your competencies such as communication, critical thinking and stress management add up. Then use the self-development career resources they provide to build your skills and become more attractive to prospective employers.

Everyday Behaviors to Aspire Towards

There will come a time when you realize that your attitude and behavior are key to how you are perceived and embraced. When people trust you, you never have to wonder, and when they follow you, always do the right thing. The behaviors below are essential to achieving personal growth and a positive mindset.

- Optimism: Be hopeful, encouraged, and believe situations can be resolved as a result of your actions.

- Inspiration: Find inspirational and motivational quotes. Memorize and say them every day.

- Empathy: Treat your feelings and the feelings of others with dignity and understanding.

- Listening: Give others your full attention without judgement.

- Celebrate: Do not take your achievements for granted. Enjoy, honor, and praise your achievements, even if no else seems to notice.

- Love: Love what you do, who you are, and give love without expectations of receiving it back.

- Giving: Give back to your peers, community, and others in need.

Workforce Preparation

Throughout your career you will be faced with many situations that will challenge various aspects of your career development, particularly grit and outcomes. Both of these components are vitally important and having one without the other can play a vital role in your decision-making. Employees with grit achieve results that transcend everyday organizational imperatives. Employees that begin planning and strategizing with outcomes in mind tend to make great decisions and are often viewed as visionaries and leaders. Employers today want you to critically think (problem-solving).

Build Empathetic Relationships

- Effective leaders are empathetic toward their employees.

- Demonstrate empathy one-on-one.

- Show genuine appreciation to peers and employees as individuals.

- To build trust do what you say and say what you mean.

Demonstrate Excitement

- If you show excitement in what you do you will ignite excitement in others.

- Employees will see and understand what drives you.

- Passion reminds you and shows others why you are doing what you do.

Emotional Intelligence

- Demonstrate the skill to control your emotional state.

- Show the ability to actively and effectively listen as if you were in others' shoes.

- Show appreciation for people's efforts, no matter how difficult the situation or conversation.

Paying Yourself First

- We all get up every day and serve others in some capacity. But the reality is that if we don't care about ourselves, our own reputations, and our own personal brands, it's a given that nobody else will. So you have to resolve to pay yourself first and give yourself the time and attention you need to create and develop your own personal brand. Doing that will pay you back tenfold over time.

Performance Accountability

- Accept responsibility for the outcomes expected of you.

- Establish a structure for accomplishing goals.

- Ask yourself what you can do to improve the situation—make a difference—and do it.

Take on Leadership Roles

- Making time to take on leadership roles is important to your brand and to your career. As you're thinking of your leadership goals and what roles might help you accomplish them, don't join ten groups, join two. And make sure you can be a leader in one of them.

Active Listening

- Give full attention to what is being said, not what you want to hear. Don't be compelled to answer someone's question midway through their sentence. Just listen.

- Allow people to tell their whole story. Ask them for permission to recall or summarize what you heard to demonstrate that you were engaged.

Make Yourself the Focal Point

- As you are developing your personal brand one of the most important things you need to think about is your network. This is what allows you to spread the word about who you are and what you can do.

Dealing with Conflict

- Consider additional ways that the situation could have been handled. Sometimes we don't consider positive intent and as a result we misunderstand someone's intention.

- Always focus on the problem, not the person. This process brings everything back to reality.

- Ask colleagues what they would do if they were in your shoes. This can help you look at things with a different view.

- Ask yourself how everything would be if it were going well (in a perfect world).

Convey Your Authority

- All too often we fail to get recognition because our credibility is either undefined or people are uncertain. Think through ways to convey your authority so that people understand the expertise you are bringing to the table. Develop your credibility.

Career Growth

- Ask yourself what your career would look like if you couldn't fail. At times we forget to dream. This question will allow you to think outside of your current state.

- Remember the types of creative things you are good at, but do not get paid for. This thinking can open up thoughts that were never considered before.

- Ask yourself what your ideal career would look like. This will make you consider the choices you've made or are considering.

- Think about what motivates you to achieve your goals (personal or professional). Motivation creates action, action creates opportunities.

Move Where the Trend is Going

- Put yourself where the trend is going. Find something, a niche, where there is growth and learn everything you can about it, write about it, and get the momentum you need to build your name and reputation as an authority on that topic. This allows you to move where the trend is going.

Be Willing to Abandon Your Strengths

- One key to success is to not be afraid to give up what has worked well in the past. What will help you get to where you want to be? Are there strengths you need to walk away from? Other areas you need to focus on and/or learn more about? If so, start formulating a plan to make that happen.

Websites for Success

The resources below will provide you with a plethora of insight and knowledge.

LinkedIn.com - Create a strong professional network

coursera.org - Take the world's best courses online

www.edx.org - Online Course from top universities

harvardx.harvard.edu - Online courses, research, blog

www.futurelearn.com - Online courses

https://www.bls.gov/audience/jobseekers.htm - Bureau of Labor Statistics

http://www.hoovers.com - Industry analysis and company profiles

khanacademy.org - Tutoring on just about everything; stay learned

https://www.roberthalf.com/salary-guide - Robert Half is the world's largest specialized staffing firm

http://www.iftf.org/home/ - Institute for the Future (IFTF) brings people together to make the future—today

https://www.mindtools.com - Career tools

https://www.nationalservice.gov - Nonprofit work opportunities

Inspirational TED Talks

TED is a media organization which posts motivational and knowledge-based talks online under the slogan "Ideas worth spreading."

- Tita Gray—My Greatest Fears Created My Strongest Values. https://www.youtube.com/watch?v=tmIiyC9n1eU

- Scott Dinsmore—How to Find Work You Love. www.ted.com/talks/scott_dinsmore_how_to_find_work_you_love

- Ken Robinson—Do Schools Kill Creativity? www.ted.com/talks/ken_robinson_says_schools_kill_creativity

- Amy Cuddy—Your Body Language May Shape Who You Are. www.ted.com/talks/amy_cuddy_your_body_language_shapes_who_you_are

- Simon Sinek—How Great Leaders Inspire Action. www.ted.com/talks/simon_sinek_how_great_leaders_inspire_action

- Brené Brown—The Power of Vulnerability. www.ted.com/talks/brene_brown_on_vulnerability

- Julian Treasure—How to Speak So That People Listen. www.ted.com/talks/julian_treasure_how_to_speak_so_that_people_want_to_listen

- Dan Pink—The Puzzle of Motivation. www.youtube.com/watch?v=rrkrvAUbU9Y

- Drew Dudley—Everyday Leadership. www.ted.com/talks/drew_dudley_everyday_leadership

Cool-Ass Podcasts

Freakonomics Radio—Explores "the hidden side of everything," telling stories about cheating schoolteachers and eating champions while teaching us all to think a bit more creatively, rationally, and productively.

Manager Tools—Each week discusses specific actions for professionals to take to achieve their desired management and career objectives.

How To Do Everything—Listeners can ask the two hosts *any* question, no matter how simple or how unusual.

TED Radio Hour—Each show features segments of several TED talks in addition to rich conversations with the speakers who gave them, all revolving around a shared idea.

Tiny Leaps, Big Changes—Focuses on habits you can develop in your everyday life to lead to a bigger change.

The Read—Info on hip hop and pop culture.

Stuff You Should Know—Listen if you want to learn about a range of topics in a new way.

Suggested Reading

The 5 Second Rule – Transform Your Life, Work, and Confidence with Everyday Courage.

The Secret – A great book for learning the importance of changing how you think.

The Mindset – Makes you evaluate yourself based on two mindsets— the fixed mindset and the growth mindset.

Outliers – One of the most compelling books of stories of success that I have ever read. This is about people that do things that are out of the ordinary.

Non-Violent Communication – NVC is based on the idea that all human beings have the capacity for compassion and only resort to violence or behavior that harms others when they don't recognize more effective strategies for meeting needs.

The Wisdom of Crowds – Demonstrates that under most circumstances, groups are remarkably intelligent and are often smarter than the smartest people in them.

The Student Leadership Challenge – Five practices for becoming an exemplary leader.

Thinking, Fast and Slow – The basic idea is simple: there are two routes to persuasion, based on two basic modes of thinking—intuitive and rational.

The Four Agreements – Rooted in traditional Toltec wisdom beliefs, four agreements in life are essential steps on the path to personal freedom.

You Are a Badass – How to Stop Doubting Your Greatness and Start Living an Awesome Life.

The Power of Habit – Why We Do What We Do in Life and Business.

Finding Flow – Describes ideas on how to live life to the fullest without wasting time and potential.

The 7 Habits of Highly Successful People – You can never go wrong with a Stephen Covey classic. This book provides life lessons that are every day affirmations.

Who Moved My Cheese? – The text describes changing one's work and life and four typical reactions to those changes.

Start with Why – How great leaders inspire everyone to take action.

The Subtle Art of Not Giving a F*ck: A Counterintuitive Approach to Living a Good Life – A much-needed grab-you-by-the-shoulders-and-look-you-in-the-eye moment of real talk, filled with entertaining stories and profane, ruthless, humor. The book is a refreshing slap for a generation to help them lead contented, grounded lives.

Eight

Top Industries

An industry is a category that refers to groups of companies that are associated based on their primary business activity. As you research industries keep in mind that certain industries are more prevalent in particular locations. For example:

- Computers and electronics manufacturing industry: California

- Tourism and hospitality industry: California and Florida

- Ambulatory health care services industry: Alabama and Arkansas

- Oil and gas extraction industry: Alaska and Colorado

- Insurance industry: Connecticut, Delaware, and Illinois

- Broadcasting and telecommunications industry: Georgia, New York, and Pennsylvania

- Accommodations industry: Hawaii and Nevada

- Chemical products manufacturing industry: Indiana and North Carolina

- Petroleum and coal products manufacturing industry: Louisiana

- Hospitals and nursing and residential care facilities industry: Maine and Massachusetts

- Federal Reserve banks and credit services: New York and South Dakota

- Publishing industries, except internet (includes software): Washington State

I know that it can be challenging to think of moving away from home or relocating, but some states offer 70K to 80K for entry level positions. In addition, depending on what industry you are considering, many companies will offer you exceptional opportunities for growth if you accept a job in a smaller metropolitan area. My suggestion is that you do your homework and consider getting an internship away from home.

Some of the 2017 top industries are listed below along with an extensive listing of national and global industries.

Green Construction

Health Care

Automation

Biomedical Engineering

Tourism

Veterinary Technology

Physical Therapy

Franchising

Education and Training

Alphabetical Listing of Industries

This section provides a list of industries and sector. Please take the time to research industries carefully and with meaning.

Abortion Policy/Anti-Abortion
Abortion Policy/Pro-Abortion Rights
Accountants
Advertising/Public Relations
Aerospace, Defense Contractors
Agribusiness
Agricultural Services and Products
Agriculture
Air Transport
Air Transport Unions
Airlines
Alcoholic Beverages
Alternative Energy Production and Services
Architectural Services

Attorneys/Law Firms
Auto Dealers
Auto Manufacturers
Automotive

Banking, Mortgage
Banks, Commercial
Banks, Savings and Loans
Bars and Restaurants
Beer, Wine and Liquor
Books, Magazines and Newspapers
Broadcasters, Radio/TV
Builders/General Contractors
Builders/Residential
Building Materials and Equipment
Building Trade Unions
Business Associations
Business Services

Cable and Satellite TV Production and Distribution
Car Dealers
Car Dealers, Imports
Car Manufacturers
Casinos/Gambling
Cattle Ranchers/Livestock
Chemical and Related Manufacturing
Chiropractors
Civil Servants/Public Officials
Clergy and Religious Organizations
Clothing Manufacturing
Coal Mining
Colleges, Universities, and Schools
Commercial Banks
Commercial TV and Radio Stations
Communications/Electronics
Computer Software
Conservative/Republican
Construction
Construction Services
Construction Unions
Credit Unions
Crop Production and Basic Processing
Cruise Ships and Lines

Dairy
Defense
Defense, Aerospace
Defense, Electronics
Defense/Foreign Policy Advocates
Dentists
Doctors and Other Health Professionals
Drug Manufacturers

Education
Education, For-profit
Electric Utilities
Electronics, Defense Contractors
Electronics, Manufacturing and Equipment
Energy and Natural Resources
Entertainment
Environmental

Farm Bureaus
Farming
Finance/Credit Companies
Finance, Insurance, and Real Estate
Food and Beverage
Food Processing and Sales
Food Products Manufacturing
Food Stores
Foreign and Defense Policy
Forestry and Forest Products
Foundations, Philanthropists, and Non-profits
Funeral Services

Gambling and Casinos
Gambling, Indian Casinos
Garbage Collection/Waste Management
Gas and Oil
Gay and Lesbian Rights and Issues
General Contractors
Government Employee Unions
Government Employees
Gun Control
Gun Rights

Health
Health Professionals
Health Services/HMOs
Hedge Funds
HMOs and Health Care Services
Home Builders
Hospitals and Nursing Homes
Hotels, Motels, and Tourism
Human Rights

Ideological/Single-issue
Indian Gaming
Industrial Unions
Insurance
Internet

Labor
Lawyers and Lobbyists
Lawyers, Law Firms
Leadership PACs (Political Action Committees)
Liquor, Wine, and Beer
Livestock
Lobbyists
Lodging/Tourism
Logging, Timber, and Paper Mills

Manufacturing, Miscellaneous
Marine Transport
Meat Processing and Products
Medical Supplies
Mining
Miscellaneous Manufacturing and Distributing
Miscellaneous Unions
Miscellaneous Defense
Miscellaneous Services
Mortgage Bankers and Brokers
Motion Picture Production and Distribution
Music Production

Natural Gas Pipelines
Newspaper, Magazine, and Book Publishing
Non-profits, Foundations, and Philanthropists
Nurses

Nursing Homes/Hospitals
Nutritional and Dietary Supplements

Oil and Gas
Other

Payday Lenders
Pharmaceutical Manufacturing
Pharmaceuticals/Health Products
Philanthropy
Phone Companies
Physicians and Other Health Professionals
Politics
Postal Unions
Poultry and Eggs
Power Utilities
Printing and Publishing
Prisons, For-profit
Private Equity and Investment Firms
Professional Sports, Sports Arenas, and Related Equipment
    and Services
Public Employees
Public Sector Unions
Publishing and Printing

Radio/TV Stations
Railroads
Real Estate
Record Companies/Singers
Recorded Music and Music Production
Recreation/Live Entertainment
Religious Organizations/Clergy
Residential Construction
Restaurants and Drinking Establishments
Retail Sales
Savings and Loans
Schools/Education
Sea Transport
Securities and Investment
Special Trade Contractors
Sports, Professional
Steel Production
Stock Brokers/Investment

Student Loan Companies
Sugar Cane and Sugar Beets

Teachers' Unions
Teachers/Education
Telecom Services and Equipment
Telephone Utilities
Textiles
Timber, Logging, and Paper Mills
Tobacco
Transportation
Transportation Unions
Trash Collection/Waste Management
Trucking
TV/Movies/Music
TV Production

Unions
Unions, Airline
Unions, Building Trades
Unions, Industrial
Unions, Miscellaneous
Unions, Public Sector
Unions, Teacher
Unions, Transportation
Universities, Colleges, and Schools

Vegetables and Fruits
Venture Capital

Waste Management
Wine, Beer, and Liquor
Women's Issues

Nine

Conclusion

Live it until you become it!

We all have a journey to trek that I call the roller coaster of life. Most times you don't know what to expect, but you strap in and know that at some point you will get to a destination. There isn't one best practice for pursuing your career, but having a better understanding of yourself is one thing over which you have complete control. How you think, how you study, how you pray, how you meditate, choice of friends, what you eat, etc., are things that you can control and they are all necessary as you decide how your journey will flow. Ghandi said,

> *"your beliefs become your thoughts,*
> *your thoughts become your words,*
> *your words become your actions,*
> *your actions become your habits,*
> *your habits become your values,*
> *your values become your destiny."*

As you are learning who you want to become and what you want to practice remember that you are perfect and imperfect just as you are. You are unique for a reason and the universe is waiting for your contributions to make this world a better place. One of the best ways to do that is by enjoying the things you do in life to the fullest. You will be challenged, you will be hurt (just decide on who is worth being hurt by), you will be disappointed, you will make mistakes, and you will be judged...just never forget that you are important and worthy of success. Keep people around you that make you laugh, inspire you, love you, and will be there to pick you up when you fall.

There are several pathways to fulfillment. Find yours. Is it working for others, being an entrepreneur, working from home, being a stay at home parent? All are great ways to live and they are all interchangeable. You don't have to aspire to one career; go after as many as you want. Just have a purpose and meaning behind what you are doing.

Acknowledgement

Dr. Luke Wood my Chair, my rock, my inspiration—thanks with all my heart. You said yes on my defense, you have given me countless recommendations, and you referred me to Montezuma Publishing. How can I ever put in words my love for you for believing in me.

To my SDSU students—everything I have ever done in academia has been for you or as a result of you. This book was written for you because of the countless moments spent with you in and out of the classroom. Big shout out to Delta Sigma Pi my brothers, Black Business Society, Aztec Music Group, Sports Business Initiative, Aztecs Out in Business, ASU, AS, and all of the other amazing student organizations at SDSU.

To the students whom I had the pleasure of teaching—I learned more from you than you can ever imagine. Thanks for the Lollipop Moments! To my RA's and students from Tenochca and South Campus Plaza, and my Peer Advisors I love you always. Aleksey, Ronald, Cooper, Pheobe, J. Cole, Alexis, Cynthia, Alex, Gabby, Taylor, Trevor, Nick G., Jordan, Javon, Tia, Ahjalee, Jesse, Mariah, Courtney, Elle, Ryan, Celeste, Brandon, Asha, Ayesha, Miya, Channelle, Karina, Krystal, Anthony, Clara, and Drew, we shared extra special moments together laughing crying, or just hanging out over a meal, much love. The moments with you gave me the inspiration to finally write this book. I hope that I haven't left anyone out, please know that it wasn't my intent. The SDSU family gave me so much that it would take a chapter to say thank you to all of the deserving students and administrators that have made a difference in my life. Big up to MC7, Kara, James, Bobbie, Jessica, Bre, the Assistant Deans, & my former Advising Staff.

Finally, thanks to my family and friends. Mom for never telling me I couldn't. Angie for being the 'lil sister that I always wanted. Aatif my big bro love you and the fam to the moon and back. To my cousins that always encouraged and cheered me on. My close friends Tina, Renee, Stephon, Nadine, Shannon, Kirsten, LeRoy, Jessica, Quinnetta, Edwin, Christina - ride or die for life thanks for holding me up.

Much Love,
Tita